REBEL GIRLS

Little Library

10+ Women who Love Animals

This is a work of creative nonfiction. It is a collection of heartwarming and thought-provoking stories inspired by the lives and adventures of influential women. It is not an encyclopedic account of the events and accomplishments of their lives.

www.rebelgirls.com

Rebel Girls, Inc.
421 Elm Ave.
Larkspur, CA 94939

Text by Dinah Dunn
Art direction by Giulia Flamini
Graphic design by Kristen Brittain
Graphic design and additional illustrations: Alessandro Raimondo
Portrait illustrations: 4: Annalisa Ventura, 8: Alice Beniero,
12: Shiane Salabie, 16: Bodil Jane, 20: Emmanuelle Walker,
24: Amanda Hall, 28: Jui Talukder, 32: Melissa Fernández Nitsche,
36: Janie Secker, 40: Angela Acevedo Perez

Printed in China, 2023
10 9 8 7 6 5 4 3 2 1
ISBN: 979-8-88964-078-3

FSC
www.fsc.org
MIX
Paper | Supporting responsible forestry
FSC™ C018179

CONTENTS

Bindi Irwin

Conservationist

Born July 24, 1998 | Australia

Once there was a girl named Bindi who lived in a zoo. Her dad, Steve, was a famous animal expert. He started the Australia Zoo Wildlife Hospital with her mom. Bindi woke up every morning to cute koalas, singing birds, and hissing snakes.

Bindi loved caring for animals big and small. Her dad loved it too. She was even named after her dad's favorite crocodile! Her dad taught her to work hard, try your best, and believe in yourself. He would tell her, "Bindi, remember you have to treat animals as you'd like to be treated."

Bindi's best friend in the zoo was a black-and-white goose named Maggie. Bindi thought she could learn to fly like her friend. Bindi never flew, but she did spend a lot of time climbing trees with her brother.

When she was eight years old, her dad died. Her family was so sad. Bindi spoke about her love for him in front of millions of people on TV. She said she planned to help animals, just like he did.

And she kept her promise. A year later, Bindi had her own TV show called *Bindi the Jungle Girl*. The show taught people how they could protect animals.

Today, Bindi works at the zoo. She and her team take care of all kinds of creatures, from kangaroos to tree frogs. They have helped more than 120,000 animals!

After all this time, the girl who grew up at the zoo is still saving wildlife. "I'm proud every day to be part of something so much bigger than myself," she says.

SCAN TO HEAR MORE!

The Black Mambas

Rangers

Formed in 2013 | South Africa

There is a huge park in the South African savanna called Balule Nature Reserve. It is home to amazing wildlife, such as lions, elephants, buffalo, and hyenas. People travel from all over the world to see the animals there.

But the park warden had a problem. Hunters were sneaking into the park. They would kill rhinos and sell their horns for a lot of money. So many rhinos were killed that there weren't a lot left. One of the oldest animals in the world might disappear!

So the warden put together a team of women rangers to stop them. He called the team the Black Mambas.

The women learned to survive in the dry, hot land known as the savanna. They became good at spotting animal traps. They learned what to do when they ran into dangerous animals.

"The Mambas are the eyes and ears of the reserve," said ranger Felicia Mogahane. While the hunters carry guns, the Black Mambas have only pepper spray. When they spot a hunter, they hide and call for help on their walkie-talkies.

The Black Mambas are proud of their work. They visit schools and teach kids about why they protect rhinos. "We don't want children to think wildlife is something you only see on TV, not in real life," said ranger Cute Mhlongo.

They also plan trips for kids to the park. "How can you value and care for something you've never seen?" asked ranger Lewyn Maefala. Once kids have seen the animals, they realize why they are worth protecting.

In the first year, the Black Mambas stopped many hunters from entering the park. Now years go by without a rhino being killed. The Black Mambas are heroes of the savanna.

Earyn McGee

Science Educator

Born September 1994 | USA

Earyn was walking in the rocky Chiricahua Mountains of Arizona, looking for a lizard. She studied reptiles in college. She was trying to find a Yarrow's spiny lizard that she had captured before. She hoped to see the bright-orange number 5 she had painted on its back.

When Earyn finally spotted the lizard, it took off like a rocket! Earyn hopped over logs and rocks, trying to catch up. The lizard's skin changed colors to help it hide. That made it hard for Earyn to spot.

What if I've lost it? Earyn thought. Then she saw a flash of orange on a tree. And there was the lizard!

She snapped a photo and posted it online. "Look at this girl!" she wrote.

To her surprise, people couldn't find the lizard in the photo. Even with the orange mark on its back, it was tricky to spot. That gave Earyn a great idea: a game on social media called #FindThatLizard.

Every week, Earyn posts a photo to see who can spot the hidden critter. After people find the lizard, she shares fun facts about it. Her thousands of fans now call her the "lizard lady."

Earyn was always interested in animals. Her family thought it was weird. But Earyn knew better. She wants to show people that creatures like lizards are fascinating. She hopes her game will get other young people of color interested in jobs studying nature. So she is doing it one hidden lizard at a time.

Ornithologist

April 13, 1868–November 25, 1929 | Germany and Brazil

Emilie was excited to start at the University of Berlin. She had taught children and saved money for years to be able go to college. It was her childhood dream to study nature. The only problem? Women couldn't go to college in Germany in 1900. But that didn't stop her.

Emilie was finally allowed to go, but there were a lot of rules. She had to come to class early and sit behind a screen, so no one could see her. She wasn't allowed to ask questions. Emilie followed the rules so she could learn. When she graduated, she began work at the Berlin Natural History Museum.

But a bigger adventure was waiting. In 1905, Emilie was hired by a museum in Brazil, halfway around the world. When she got on the boat for her journey, it was the first time she had traveled so far away.

From then on, Brazil was Emilie's home. She was both a scientist and an explorer. She studied the birds of the Amazon. She bravely went deep into the rain forest to find birds no one had seen before. She found many new ones. She sent more than 10,000 birds and animals to museums all over the world.

Once, someone asked if she ever was afraid during her travels. Emilie replied, "That is no way for a German to think!"

On one boat trip, she put her hand in the water and a fish bit her hand.

Soon it became infected. There were no doctors to help her. She had to cut off part of her own finger!

When Emilie left the rain forest, she wrote a book about birds that was 530 pages long. At least five animals, including two birds, have been named after the brave scientist.

Primatologist

Born April 3, 1934 | UK

Once there was a girl in England named Jane. She loved climbing trees and reading books. Her dream was to go to Africa and learn about wild animals.

When she was 26 years old, Jane traveled to the country of Tanzania. Her plan was to study chimpanzees where they lived. Some scientists watched them from far away. Others studied chimps in cages. Jane wanted to learn by getting chimps in the wild to trust her.

At first, it was hard. The chimps would run away when they saw her. But Jane kept visiting the same place every day at the same time. Over time, the chimps got used to her.

Getting closer was not enough for Jane. She wanted to become friends with them. So she started a "banana club." Whenever she visited the chimpanzees, she would share bananas with them. She climbed trees and ate the same foods they ate. Soon, the chimps treated Jane like a friend.

Jane learned that chimps were more like humans than scientists knew. They could make tools. They showed emotions, such as happiness and sadness. They even talked to each other, using 120 different sounds.

Once, Jane found a chimpanzee that was hurt. She helped it get better. Before it went back into the wild, the chimpanzee gave her a long hug goodbye. Jane was thrilled. She had earned the chimps' trust!

Now Jane travels the world, telling people about her chimpanzee friends. She's written books about her time in Tanzania. She even started a program called Roots & Shoots. It teaches kids to help nature and their communities.

SCAN TO HEAR MORE!

Maria Sibylla Merian

Naturalist

April 2, 1647–January 13, 1717 | Germany

Maria was a little girl who loved art. Every day, she would paint flowers. Sometimes, she found caterpillars climbing on the flowers she observed. She made paintings of how they slowly changed into beautiful butterflies. At that time, people thought butterflies grew in mud like plants. Maria knew better, but no one believed her.

Years passed. Maria became a great nature painter. Most artists at that time would kill a creature in order to paint it. But Maria tried to paint animals, bugs, and plants where they lived. Her books and paintings were beautiful, but not many people saw them.

One day, Maria visited a museum in the Netherlands. It was filled with amazing insects found in South America. Maria thought, *If I could study insects there, I could write a book that people would notice*. So at the age of 52, she and her youngest daughter made the dangerous trip to the South American rain forest. They traveled 5,000 miles by boat.

For two years, Maria studied, drew, and painted in the rain forest. She climbed tall trees to study the bugs. She saw how caterpillars turned into butterflies. She carefully painted everything she saw.

Lots of Maria's paintings showed creatures doing things no one had ever seen before. One painting showed a giant spider eating a small bird. Another showed ants that worked together to build a bridge with their bodies.

Maria got sick, so she returned to the Netherlands. There, she put together a book showing all she had learned. Her daughter helped color the art. It was a huge success.

Scientists used it to learn more about insects and other animals. Thanks to Maria, they finally understood that butterflies didn't grow in mud!

Purnima Devi Barman

Wildlife Biologist

Birthdate Unknown | India

When Purnima was five years old, she was sent to live with her grandmother. She didn't want to go! She couldn't stop crying. Her grandmother didn't know what to do. So she took Purnima to the fields and the river to show her the birds. *Listen to the bird songs!* her grandmother said. *Sing for the egrets and the storks.* Purnima fell in love with birds.

Purnima's neighbors didn't feel the same way, especially about storks. They saw storks as dirty pests that brought bad luck. But Purnima saw something different. She saw beautiful birds that helped the planet.

In India, there is a huge stork known as the *hargila*. Its name

means “bone swallower.” It will eat just about anything, including dead animals. When the hargila eat, they also clean up the environment.

But some people think the birds are gross because their nests and poop smell awful. People do not want them in their yards. Sadly, many birds were killed. Soon, there weren’t many left in the world.

Purnima was in college when she got a call from a fellow bird lover. *Help!* A man was cutting down trees with hargila nests in them. Baby birds were falling to the ground! Purnima rushed to try to save them. The man yelled at her and told her to go away.

How can I make everyone understand how important these birds are? she wondered. So she created songs and shows about this special stork. Then, Purnima asked women around her region for help. Now there are more than 10,000 women in the Hargila Army. They care for hurt birds and watch over nests. They make yarn crafts that show the beautiful birds. And now people have learned to love the hargila!

Shaine Kilyun

Pet-Wheelchair Maker

Born September 16, 2005 | USA

Shaine loved all creatures, big and small. She had a dog, two cats, a guinea pig, and a turtle of her own. Shaine also helped out at animal hospitals. Still, she wanted to do more. But what?

One day, Shaine came across a YouTube video about how to make a wheelchair for a dog. *What a great way to do something for animals in need!* Shaine thought. She was a little worried that no one would trust a 15-year-old to make their dog a wheelchair. But she had to try.

Shaine bought all her supplies. She made a design. Then she got to work. After she built the first wheelchair, she showed it to a veterinarian to make sure she did it right. Then she went on Instagram with her new project. She called her account Wheelies.

On Instagram, people reached out to Shaine. *Can you make a wheelchair for my dog?* they asked. Soon Shaine was busy making more. She shared photos and videos of some of the animals she helped. After a few months, she was making wheelchairs for pets all around the world. It made her so happy to help animals in need.

She's made large wheelchairs for Labradors and tiny wheelchairs for Chihuahuas. She's built wheelchairs for cats, a hedgehog, and even a duck! She loves to see these animals run and play.

She gave most of her wheelchairs to animal shelters for free. Her wheelchairs have made it possible for many animals that had trouble moving to find loving homes. "I truly want to make a difference for as many animals as I possibly can," Shaine says.

Temple Grandin

Professor of Animal Sciences

Born August 29, 1947 | USA

Once upon a time, there was a girl named Temple who didn't speak until she was three and a half years old. Instead, she would scream and hum. Her mom took her to doctors to figure out what was happening. They didn't know! It wasn't until Temple was older that she learned she was autistic.

Autistic people's brains make them see and feel the world differently. Like many autistic children, Temple didn't like to be hugged. But she loved the feeling of being pressed. So in college, she invented a machine that could hug her just the way she wanted.

At that time, many people didn't understand autism. They didn't realize that not all autistic people were the same. Temple helped the world understand by talking about her autism. She explained the different way her brain worked. "I think in pictures," she liked to say. "I don't think in language."

Temple believes her autism helps her understand animals. They don't think in words either. Temple also noticed that autistic people and animals are sometimes afraid of the same things. A high noise, a quick movement, or a piece of paper blowing in the wind could be scary.

This understanding has led her to study animals. Temple worked with farmers who raised cows for meat to make the cows' final days easier. She also helped make sure they are treated fairly. She said, "The most important thing for an animal is the quality of its life." She has written books and worked with big companies to make animals' lives better.

SCAN TO HEAR MORE!

Veterinarian

Born May 10, 1965 | USA

Tolani grew up around animals. On her tribe's reservation in New Mexico, her father raised cattle, sheep, and horses. So did her grandfathers and her great-grandfather, like many of her Laguna tribe.

"I always had a dog, a cat, and a horse," she said. "Any critter I could bring home and save, I was always trying to do that." When she was 15 years old, she saw a sheep hurt while it was getting its wool cut off. There was nothing she could do to help. From that moment on, she knew she'd be a veterinarian.

At veterinary school, Tolani wasn't like other people in her class. Sure, she loved cats and dogs. But she also loved cows. And she wasn't afraid to look after big animals, such as horses, bison, and elk. Some can weigh as much as pickup trucks! But they still need to be seen by a doctor, just like pets and people do. And that's where Tolani comes in.

Tolani's work has taken her around the world. She has spent time caring for bison and elk in Yellowstone National Park. She looks into their mouths, listens to their hearts, and takes their temperatures. She's treated sickness in cattle and sheep in Bolivia and the

United Kingdom. And now she works to protect wild horses and burros as part of the US Forest Service.

Like many people in her tribe, Tolani raises cattle and horses. She also has three dogs and six cats. She even started an animal hospital on her reservation, just like she dreamed when she was a kid.

SCAN TO HEAR MORE!

About Rebel Girls

Rebel Girls is a global, multi-platform empowerment brand dedicated to helping raise the most inspired and confident generation of girls through content, experiences, products, and community. Originating from an international best-selling children's book, Rebel Girls amplifies stories of real-life women throughout history, geography, and field of excellence. With a growing community of nearly 20 million self-identified Rebel Girls spanning more than 100 countries, the brand engages with Generation Alpha through its book series, award-winning podcast, events, and merchandise. With the 2021 launch of the Rebel Girls app, the company has created a flagship destination for girls to explore a wondrous world filled with inspiring true stories of extraordinary women.

As a B Corp, we're part of a global community of businesses that meet high standards of social and environmental impact.

Join the Rebel Girls community:

Facebook: facebook.com/rebelgirls
Instagram: @rebelgirls
Twitter: @rebelgirlsbook
TikTok: @rebelgirlsbook
Web: rebelgirls.com
Podcast: rebelgirls.com/podcast
App: rebelgirls.com/audio

If you liked this book, please take a moment to review it wherever you prefer!